Constitutiional Independent Presentation

A State Ratified Federal Limit
Amendment, Need A 3rd Party?
Constitutional Federal Government

By: B. J. Galt

American Success

America represents a unique, shining example in government. Its success is the envy of people all over the world. World economies depend on US success.

Annual Gross Domestic Production:

United States $15.5 Trillion

China $5.8 Trillion

Japan $5.4 Trillion

United Kingdom $3.5 Trillion

Germany $3.2 Trillion

France $2.5 Trillion

US is > China, Japan, UK, Germany combined.

Military Support

Many countries depend on America for
military and economic support.
Where in the world is our Military?
On 700+ bases in 135 nations
The 2013 Military Budget was $530 Billion
excluding Iraq and Afghaniston war costs.
The United States military budget
accounts for 40% of the world's
military spending.

Atlas America

America is truly Atlas to the world

Will Atlas have to shrug?

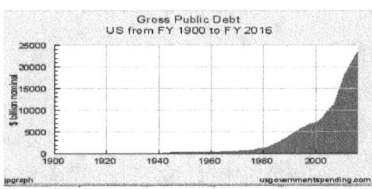

The 2013 Federal debt is $17+ Trillion. Continuing Deficit spending adds to the debt every year. Insolvency due to required debt interest payments is a real possibility.

Republican Spending

President Bush added to the debt problem by never
vetoing any Republican spending bill.
He authorized the Iraq and Afghanistan wars,
the Part D Medication program, the Economic
Stimulus Act of 2008 and the TARP bank
bailout, all without budget funding, allowing
unprecedented deficits to be created.
The Republicans lost their reputation as the
party of constitutional small government and
low taxes.

Democratic Spending

In the first years of the Obama administration, using congressional majorities and the Presidency, the $800 Billion American Recovery and Reinvestment Act of 2009 was passed without funding to stimulate the economy. This added to the Federal Deficit in that year. It did little to eliminate the recession. It did increase federal and state spending.

The ACA

The Obama administration and Democratic congressional majority passed the 2500 page Affordable Care Act (Obama Care) without any Republican support.

This has future implications of massive increases in taxes, Federal controls, bureaucracies and related health costs.

Unbalanced Budget Proposals

Democrat or Republican budget plans only reduce the amount of budget growth, not current spending. Future legislators must do the actual cutting to reduce deficits and debt growth.

 None of the plans reduce the $17 Trillion current national debt. Over the next 10 year period, $7 – 8 Trillion will be added to the debt. How Long before funding realities will force insolvency?

How will our children deal with these generational debt burdens?

The Peter Principle

The Peter Principle states; "In a bureaucracy, everyone tends to rise to their level of incompetence, then they are no longer promoted. In time, every post tends to be occupied by an incompetent employee."

This principle and problem is very true in government as well as the private sector . Federal employee protective unions make this problem even greater.

A Limit To Size?

"To the size of a state there is a limit, as there is to plants, animals and implements, for they can not retain their facility when they are too large."

Aristotle

A Tipping Point

The critical point is when the number of people living on government entitlements passes 50% and can control future elections.

Today, 45% of US citizens pay no income taxes.

The Democratic party has majority support from all minorities, welfare recipients, unions, and government workers making it difficult for anyone to propose any reduction in government spending or programs.

Constitutional Road Blocks

 The Constitution of the United States is unique
among the constitutions of the world in the way it
restricts the powers of the Federal Government
with checks and balances. Its allowed powers
are specifically listed in the 10th Amendment
which then states:

"The powers not delegated to the United States
by the Constitution, nor prohibited by it to the
States, are reserved to the States respectively,
or to the people."

Dollar Purchasing Power Devaluation

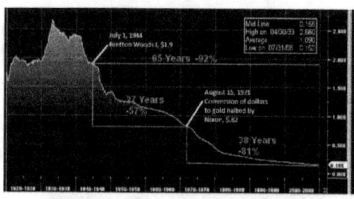

This chart shows $ devaluation up to the year 2000. How much more has the Federal Reserve devalued the dollar with Quantitative Easing (printing money) since then?

Physical Demensions Of Money

Not too long ago, a $ Billion ($ One Thousand Million) was the maximum sum used to describe most government spending.

Even $ One Billion is not clearly understood by most people.

$1 Billion = A stack of $1 bills 75 Miles high.
$1 Trillion = One Thousand Billions.

$1 BILLION in ½" packages of $10,000 of $100 bills

$1 Trillion in ½" packages of $10,000 of $100 bills

Billions And Trillions

The next time you hear politicians speak of Billion and Trillion dollar budgets and expenditures, consider the physical dimensions of the money they are proposing to spend.

When a politician says he is proposing to spend $1 Billion for a project, ask him if it is worth 1,000 Million Dollars? See if his answer shows that he really appreciates what a Billion Dollars truly represents.

Deficit And Debt Problems

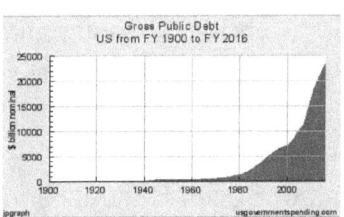

The 2013 Debt is $17+ Trillion.

Annual deficits (spending exceeding revenue) add Hundreds of Billions to the debt. By 2020 the debt will be over $20 Trillion.

Interest Payment Danger

Between 2013 and 2022, estimated interest costs which must paid from current budgets will be:

☐ higher than Medicaid spending

☐ equal to half of Social Security spending

☐ close to what is spent on all of defense

☐ Driven by rising rates to fight inflation, debt interest payment potentials represent the greatest danger leading to national insolvency.

How To Survive

To Eliminate deficits and reduce the debt to avoid national insolvency:

+Eliminate unconstitutional federal spending.

+Promote powerful growth of the national economy; Energy production, Computing Power, Nano and Graphene technology.

+Support Tax reform and regulation policies that will generate economic expansion.

Current Constitutional checks and balances are inadequate to accomplish needed change.

To reestablish a Constitutional Federal Government Consider:

A FEDERAL LIMIT AMENDMENT

The total annual expenditures of the Federal Government of the United States shall not exceed a limit established at the time of ratification of this amendment except as may be authorized at any time for periods of up to twelve months by at least fifty one percent of the State Legislatures. After ratification of this amendment, all income of the Federal Government of the United States in excess of the established expenditure limit shall be disbursed to the States on the basis of population or shall be used to reduce the national debt.

Basic disciplines created by such an amendment;

1. Control of the size and growth of the Federal Government through a constitutional budgetary limit.

2. Debt reduction or dispersion of excess federal funds in a manner that is nationally equitable and not subject to federal political influence.

3. Federal competition for available funds within the limit will increase program oversight, rejustification and the reduction and elimination of unnecessary and duplicate functions.

More Disciplines

4. State competition for available funds would add a powerful additional check and balance effect to the Federal Government.

5. The Constitutional Congressional requirement to declare war would be reinforced. The Vietnam, Iraq and Afghanistan wars would likely not have been authorized and funded with this amendment in effect.

6. States rights and constitutional federalism would be strengthened. This fact would provide a strong incentive for states to use their constitutional right to institute a Federal Limit Amendment.

States Rights

The states, in initial agreement, designed, created and ratified the Constitution of the United States. Ultimately, the states must concur that the Federal government conforms to the requirement of the US Constitution.

If the Federal Government significantly deviates from the specifications in the Constitution, Article 5 defines the right of states to propose and ratify amendments as needed.

"Ammendment ratification by ¾ of the several States or by conventions."

Energy Economic Potential

Great potential exists in expansion of energy resources. The US has the potential to become energy independent and energy rich if national policies and incentives focus on such resources.

Oil, natural gas, coal, nuclear must all be supported and promoted. Solar and wind power generation can also be supported as they develop and become economically competitive.

The Power Of Computing

Another force that will powerfully strengthen and stimulate the economy is the continuing acceleration of the speed and power of computers. Gordon Moore, a CEO of the Intel Corporation chip manufacturer stated Moore's Law.

"Over the history of computers, the number of transistors on chips doubles approximately every two years".

Moore's Law

This means that computers decrease in size and double in speed and memory capacity every 2 years. What is amazing is that this doubling of computer power is likely to continue for the foreseeable future.

The influence of this multiplying computer power has the potential to accelerate the productivity and expansion of the US economy as well as world interconnectivity.

Computer Power Integration

As computing power proliferates and is integrated into products, more control and intelligence will increase their value.

Robotics and 3D printing of parts will become more capable increasing accuracy, speed and productivity thereby vastly improving manufacturing.

As computing power is further integrated into transportation vehicles and roads, safety and efficiencies will be greatly improved.

NanoTechnology Potentials

Nanotechnology is the manipulation of matter on an atomic, molecular scale. Nanotechnology works with materials, devices, and other structures sized from 1 to 100 nanometers.

With a variety of potential applications, nanotechnology is a key technology for the future.

As micro computing is integrated with nanotechnology, many fields will evolve in ways that are incomprehensible today.

Grahpene A Wonder Material

Graphene is the world's new wonder material. It's the thinnest electronic material ever invented, consisting of a layer of carbon atoms just a single atom thick. It weighs almost nothing, only 0.77 grams for a square meter.

Graphene is 100 times stronger than steel of the same thickness. It conducts both heat and electricity better than copper, and has outstanding optical and mechanical properties. Initially this will mean that graphene is used to help improve the performance and efficiency of current materials and substances.

As nano-technology and micro computing is combined with new materials, like graphene many fields will evolve in life changing ways that are incomprehensible today.

The Future?

We are at a medieval stage in terms of intelligent use and control of government in society.

Our ability to design and implement new, functional systems of governmental control will determine whether we now move into a dark age of smothering, fiscal bankruptcy, irresponsible, socialistic over government and an eventual end to the "American dream".

No System?

If our founding principles cannot be made to work, if our people cannot make sound readjustments and maintain effective control of their government, <u>then there is no governmental system known to mankind that will not eventually be destroyed by its parental society.</u>

Fulfill This Need

Can we evaluate the past and from this evaluation reform the principles of freedom and government thereby giving a new vitality and concern to American politics?

Creative minds that can provide answers to fill the vacuum between right and left extremism constitute this nation's greatest present need. Hopefully, such a need cannot go unfulfilled.

What Legacy?

What will we pass on to our grandchildren; unfillable program promises, massive, uncontrollable government and unsustainable national debts? Will this still be a nation founded on Constitutional principles of effective government in a free society? Will Abraham Lincoln's description of America having "Government of the people, by the people and for the people" still apply? With awareness, concern and action it can be so.

Who Is B. J. Galt?

B. J. Galt is the pseudonym of a retired Computer System Engineer. He has published three books defining how end users can be designers of major applications. He originated the design of a computer software system which was responsible for >$3 Billion in system sales for a major corporation.

His book, "Atlas America" describes the author's reflections, concerns and recommendations based on over 40 years observance of large, corporate bureaucracy and political history. As a past Conservative and Republican, he now describes himself as a Constitutional Independent. The book represents his evolved, current, political perspectives. It suggests solutions to accomplish a "**recurrence to constitutional principles**".

Publishing

The document, "Constitutional Independent Presentation", summarizes the key points made in the book: "Constitutional Independent"

A State Ratified Federal Limit Amendment, Need A 3rd Party? Constitutional Federal Government

Printed copies of the presentation and the book are available at: https://www.createspace.com

Also on Kindle & at Amazon Books

Search for the Author: B. J. Galt

Email request a Free summary Video or PDF   B. J. Galt
Email: bjongalt@gmail.com